God's Masterplan For Money - A Biblical Guide To Financial Stewardship

The Stewardship Collection, Volume 2

Terence A. Townsend

Published by T.E. Publishers, 2024.

While every precaution has been taken in the preparation of this book, the publisher assumes no responsibility for errors or omissions, or for damages resulting from the use of the information contained herein.

GOD'S MASTERPLAN FOR MONEY - A BIBLICAL GUIDE TO FINANCIAL STEWARDSHIP

First edition. January 5, 2024.

Copyright © 2024 Terence A. Townsend.

Written by Terence A. Townsend.

Also by Terence A. Townsend

Healthy Eats Collection

Plant-Powered Mornings: 24 Delicious Vegan Breakfast Recipes to Start Your Day Right

The Christian Virtue Collection

The Power Of True Christian Virtue: Unleashing Your Full Potential

The Stewardship Collection

Power Of Financial Stewardship

God's Masterplan For Money - A Biblical Guide To Financial Stewardship

Watch for more at www.tefinancialservices.com.

Table of Contents

I want to dedicted this book to the people that have impacted my life in so many positive ways. From my mother, Paula Sue Townsend, who as a single parent, raised me with the understanding that dreams can be achieved through belief in God, prayer, hard-work and education. I want to also thank my bride, my diamond, the woman who gave me a family, Jacqueline Ann Townsend.

All Love, His Glory!

Introduction

I hate being broke. I know that's not the proper way to open up a book, but I really do hate being broke. One issue that I've dealt with most of my life is the fact that I have had either just enough money or never enough money.

The thing is, I have discovered that the most important aspect of us being humans is our ability to change our circumstance; meaning that our circumstance is subject to us, to our activity, to our design and desire.

"Everything that we do is birthed through challenge." - Terence André Townsend

Everything we accomplished is immersed in a struggle. The only thing that we are responsible for is how we manage or invest what we have been given. God has invested so much into us becoming who we are in Christ that all excuses for us not 'becoming' all that God created us to be, are eliminated. This is a very important point, because as I opened up with the statement I hate to be broke, in a deeper since I am definitively stating, "I hate experiencing the feeling of brokenness."

Brokenness. A condition that can be attributed to one's experiences, nurtured values and environmental observations. When people have been let down by life, struggle daily to buy basic resources for normal function or have been subjected to constant abusiveness, brokenness has a bad habit of settling into that person's psyche; having a voice that vocalizes thoughts of pessimism during moments of critical decision making. Brokenness has the ability to influence thought on new opportunities, new relationships, personal wellness, environmental suitability and as it pertains to our subject at hand, financial decision making and decisiveness.

"Everybody has a different kind of story.." lyric from theme song of the 80s sitcom, Different Strokes.

Quick Question:

"What does success look like for you in your journey? How has an inclination towards brokenness, or better stated, broken thinking, prevented you from seeing the fulfillment of God's plan for the success of your vision?"

Wealth affords us options that the disadvantaged are not privileged too. Financial decision making looks different for us all considering the momentary space we occupy. But the unbridled sentimentality of brokenness precipitates disengagement, negative attitude(s) and irrational fear driven decision making that can jeopardize the potential of any desirable outcome.

No one chooses brokenness, but too often it shares the ride. What does brokenness mean in the Bible? Brokenness, in God's eyes, is being so crushed by the sin and darkness of the world that we recognize there is no place to turn but to God. The fact is, God Himself has aligned the fulfillment of His Purpose (the purpose of man) with the manifestation of our success.

Jeremiah 29:11 NIV

For I know the plans I have for you," declares the Lord, "plans to prosper you and not to harm you, plans to give you hope and a future.

The intention of this book is to equip you with practices that 'snuff out' the influence of broken thought. I believe that by adopting, adapting and implementing these principles, you will see God's purpose being accomplished in and through your life.

Definition Of Financial Stewardship

Financial stewardship is a concept that is deeply rooted in the Bible. It is the responsibility of managing one's finances in a way that honors God and ensures that the resources entrusted to us are utilized in the best possible manner. In simpler terms, financial stewardship refers to the proper management of money and resources in a way that is consistent with biblical principles.

• • • •

THE BIBLE TEACHES ALL things belong to God, including our money and possessions. As such, we are stewards of these resources, entrusted with the responsibility of managing them wisely. Financial stewardship involves the proper use of these resources, not only for our own benefit but also for the benefit of others and the glory of God.

Biblical financial stewardship involves several key principles, including faithfulness, honesty, diligence, and generosity. We are called to be faithful stewards of the resources God has given us, using them wisely and responsibly. This means being honest in our financial dealings, avoiding debt, and living within our means. It also means being diligent in our work, using our talents and abilities to earn a living and provide for ourselves and our families.

Generosity is another important aspect of financial stewardship. The Bible teaches we are to give generously to others, both to support the work of God and to help those in need. This involves not only giving to our local church but also supporting charitable organizations and other ministries that are doing good work in the world.

Financial stewardship also involves wise planning and budgeting. We are called to be wise stewards of our resources, using them in a way that is consistent with our values and priorities. This means creating a budget and sticking to it, being intentional about our spending, and avoiding unnecessary expenses.

Finally, financial stewardship involves the proper use of debt and the wise management of investments. The Bible teaches we should avoid debt but also acknowledges that there may be times when borrowing is necessary.

When we borrow, we are called to do so wisely, avoiding high-interest loans and other forms of predatory lending. We are also called to be wise investors, using our resources to support companies and industries that align with our values and priorities.

In summary, financial stewardship is about managing our resources in a way that honors God, serves others, and promotes our own well-being. It involves faithfulness, honesty, diligence, generosity, wise planning, and prudent management of debt and investments. By embracing these principles, we can become faithful stewards of the resources God has given us and live a life of abundance and blessing.

Importance Of Financial Stewardship In Christianity

As Christians, we are called to be good stewards of the resources, God has entrusted that to us. This includes our finances. The Bible has a lot to say about the importance of financial stewardship in our lives. In fact, money and possessions are mentioned over 2,000 times in the Bible.

One of the key principles of financial stewardship is that everything we have ultimately belongs to God. We are simply managers of His resources. This means that we have a responsibility to use our money and possessions in ways that honor Him and further His kingdom.

Biblical teachings on financial stewardship go beyond just avoiding debt and budgeting wisely. They also focus on giving generously to others. In 2 Corinthians 9:7, we are reminded that *"God loves a cheerful giver."* As Christians, we are called to give sacrificially, not just out of our excess.

Tithing is another important aspect of financial stewardship in Christianity. While the practice of tithing is not specifically commanded in the New Testament, it is mentioned throughout the Old

The Bible also teaches us about the dangers of loving money and possessions too much. In 1 Timothy 6:10, we are warned that "the love of money is a root of all kinds of evil." We must guard against the temptation to make money and possessions our idols.The Bible tells us that loving money and possessions too much can be dangerous. In 1 Timothy 6:10, it says that "the love of money is a root of all kinds of evil." This is because when we love money and possessions more than we love God, it can lead us to do things we wouldn't normally do. For example, we might be tempted to lie, cheat, or steal in order to get what we want. We might also neglect our relationships with family and friends, as well as our spiritual life.

There are many ways to guard against the temptation to make money and possessions of our idols. One way is to remember that God is the only one who can truly satisfy us. No amount of money or possessions can ever fill the void in our hearts that only God can fill. Another way to guard against this temptation is to be generous with our money and possessions. When we give to others, it helps us to keep our focus on what is truly important in life. It also helps us to develop a heart of compassion for others.

We need to remember that God is always watching us. He knows our hearts, and He knows our motivations. If we are tempted to love money and possessions more than we love Him, He will not be pleased. We need to be careful not to let our love of money and possessions become an idol in our lives.

Ultimately, financial stewardship is about recognizing that our resources are not our own and using them in a way that honors God. This includes giving generously to others, tithing to support the work of the church, avoiding debt, and budgeting wisely. By following these principles, we can be good stewards of the resources that God has given us and advance His kingdom here on earth.

My Revelation:

Years ago, I was pastoring a small church that I founded. I was back in school chasing my degree in business and working temp jobs to make ends meet for the family. One Sunday morning I was ministering to our small congregation, and I received a word of knowledge as a revelation. "One day the world will be so bad that the Kingdom is going to have to take care of the Kingdom." I fully saw how the revelation and the times would play out. The government would begin pulling back its support of citizens and opportunities would grow slim. Many kingdom people would be caught unaware, unskilled and under prepared for these moments worldwide. But God would not forsake His people. He would cause Kingdom people, who at this time would have been rejected by many and subjected to criticism and oppressive practices, to discover an underground surplus of wisdom, innovation and resourcefulness. Creating a force for survival and unification amongst believers.

This revelation has stayed at the forefront of my thoughts and motivation for preaching. I believe that there is no greater opportunity that we have as humans than to get educated. Not just in how to handle money but in the sciences, communication, business, politics, in every area that affects the livelihood of mankind. We as believers are called to be on the frontline of revolutionary change, societal growth and its welfare. We are called to win and master the marketplace with love, grace and wisdom. Preparing the next generation of believers to take the stage and, with the right heart and mindset, press forward God's agenda as it is found in the Words of Jesus, *"Thy kingdom come, Thy will be done in earth, as it is in heaven."* (Matthew 6:10)

Purpose Of The Book

The purpose of this book, "God's Masterplan For Money: A Biblical Guide to Financial Stewardship," is to provide a comprehensive guide for Christians seeking to manage their finances biblically soundly. Many Christians struggle with their finances, often feeling overwhelmed and unsure of how to handle their money effectively. This book seeks to help readers understand what the Bible says about financial stewardship and to provide practical advice for managing money according to biblical principles.

One of the dominant themes of this book is the importance of financial stewardship in the Christian life. The Bible teaches that everything we have is a gift from God, and that we are called to manage these resources wisely. This includes not only our money but also our time, talents, and other resources. By learning to be good stewards of our finances, we can honor God, provide for our families, and make a positive impact on the world around us.

Throughout this book, readers will find practical advice on a variety of financial topics, including debt management, budgeting, saving and investing, and tithing. Each chapter is grounded in biblical principles and offers practical tips for managing money in a way that is consistent with the teachings of the Bible.

One of the key messages of this book is the importance of generosity and charitable giving. The Bible teaches we are called to love our neighbors as ourselves and to care for those in need. By giving generously to others, we can show this love and make a positive impact on the world.

The goal of this book is to help readers develop a biblical perspective on wealth and money. By understanding what the Bible teaches about financial stewardship, readers can make wise decisions about their finances and use their resources to honor God and serve others. Whether you are struggling with debt, seeking to save for the future, or simply looking for guidance on how to manage your finances, this book offers practical advice and biblical wisdom to help you navigate the complex world of money management.

What the Bible says about Financial Stewardship
The Biblical Perspective On Money

The biblical perspective on money is a topic that is often overlooked in modern discussions about financial stewardship. However, the Bible has a great deal to say about money and how Christians should approach it.

One of the main biblical principles regarding money is that it is ultimately God's.

1 Chronicles 29:11-12 NIV

"Yours, Lord, is the greatness and the power and the glory and the majesty and the splendor, for everything in heaven and earth is yours.

Yours, Lord, is the kingdom; you are exalted as head over all. Wealth and honor come from you; you are the ruler of all things. In your hands are strength and power to exalt and give strength to all."

This passage reminds us that everything we have, including our money and possessions, ultimately belongs to God. As such, we are called to be good stewards of what we have been given, using our resources in a way that honors God and furthers his kingdom.

Another important biblical principle regarding money is the importance of generosity. Proverbs 11:25 states, *"A generous person will prosper; whoever refreshes others will be refreshed."* Likewise, 2 Corinthians 9:7 reminds us that *"each of you should give what you have decided in your heart to give, not reluctantly or under compulsion, for God loves a cheerful giver."*

These passages emphasize the importance of giving generously and joyfully, expecting nothing in return. This is not only a way to honor God, but it is also a way to bless others and further his kingdom.

Finally, the Bible offers guidance on how to manage our money wisely. Proverbs 21:5 reminds us that *"the plans of the diligent lead to profit as surely as haste leads to poverty."* Likewise, Proverbs 22:7 warns us that *"the borrower is slave to the lender."*

These passages remind us of the importance of budgeting, saving, and avoiding debt. By managing our money wisely, we can honor God, bless others, and ensure that we can provide for ourselves and our families.

In conclusion, the biblical perspective on money offers valuable guidance for Christians seeking to be good stewards of their finances. By remembering that our money ultimately belongs to God, giving generously and joyfully, and managing our money wisely, we can honor God and further his kingdom with our resources.

Examples Of Financial Stewardship In The Bible

The Bible is replete with examples of financial stewardship that Christians can learn from. These examples show how people in ancient times managed their finances in a way that pleased God and how we can apply the same principles today.

One of the most famous examples of financial stewardship is found in the book of Genesis. After his brothers sold into slavery, After serving in Potipher's house and after a stint in prison, Joseph eventually became the second-in-command of Egypt. During a time of famine, he stored up food to prepare for the lean years. This wise planning meant that Egypt had enough food to survive the famine, and that Joseph could provide for his family when they came to him for help.

Another example of financial stewardship is found in the book of Proverbs. In Proverbs 6:6-8, we are told to consider the ways of the ant, who stores up food in the summer to prepare for the winter. This teaches us the importance of planning and being prepared for unexpected expenses.

In the New Testament, we see the example of the widow who gave two small coins to the temple treasury. While others gave large amounts of money, Jesus praised the widow's gift because it was all she had. This teaches us it's not the amount we give that matters, but the heart behind our giving.

Another example of financial stewardship is found in the parable of the talents. In this story, a man gives his servants different amounts of money to invest while he is away. Two of the servants invest the money and earn a profit, while the third servant buries his money in the ground. When the man returns, he rewards the two faithful servants and punishes the third for not using his money wisely. This teaches us the importance of using our resources wisely and investing in things that will bring a return.

These examples and many others show us that financial stewardship is an important aspect of our faith. By following the principles of the Bible and managing our finances wisely, we can honor God and provide for ourselves and our families.

The Christian's Responsibility As A Steward

As Christians, we believe that everything we have is a gift from God, and we are simply stewards of His resources. This means that we have a responsibility to manage our finances in a way that honors God and reflects His values.

One of the key principles of financial stewardship is generosity. In the Bible, we are called to give generously to those in need and to support the work of the church. This can take many forms, from tithing to charitable giving to supporting missions and other ministries.

Another important aspect of financial stewardship is budgeting and financial planning. We are called to be wise stewards of the resources God has entrusted to us, and that means setting priorities and making intentional decisions about how we use our money. This may involve making sacrifices and living within our means, but it also means that we can experience the joy of giving and the blessings that come from living a life of faith and generosity.

In addition to these practical steps, we are also called to seek God's wisdom and guidance in all areas of our financial lives. This means praying for wisdom and discernment, asking for guidance from trusted mentors and advisors, and being willing to make changes when necessary.

Ultimately, our goal as Christian stewards is not just to accumulate wealth or achieve financial success, but to use our resources to further God's kingdom and bring glory to Him. This may mean making sacrifices and taking risks, but it also means experiencing the joy and fulfillment that comes from living a life of faith and stewardship.

As we seek to follow God's calling in our lives, let us remember our finances are not just a means to an end, but a powerful tool for spreading the love and grace of Christ to those around us. May we be faithful stewards of God's resources, and may our lives be a testament to His goodness and provision.

Biblical Principles For Debt Management
The Dangers Of Debt

D ebt can be a trap that ensnares even the most financially responsible individuals. It is a dangerous cycle that is hard to break free from, and can lead to overwhelming stress and anxiety. The Bible warns us against the dangers of debt and advises us to avoid it as much as possible.

One of the fundamental problems with debt is that it puts us in a position of servitude to our creditors. Proverbs 22:7 says, *"The rich rule over the poor, and the borrower is slave to the lender."* When we owe money to someone else, we are no longer in control of our own finances. We have to work hard to pay off our debts, often sacrificing our own needs and wants in the process.

Debt can also lead to a cycle of borrowing and spending that is hard to break. When we use credit cards or take out loans to pay for things we can't afford, we are essentially living beyond our means. This can lead to a vicious cycle of debt, where we are constantly borrowing to pay off previous debts.

Debt can cause significant stress and anxiety, which can take a toll on our physical and emotional health. When we are constantly worried about paying off our debts, it can affect our relationships, work performance, and overall quality of life.

As Christians, we are called to be good stewards of the resources that God has entrusted to us. This means being responsible for our finances, avoiding debt and living within our means. Proverbs 21:20 says, *"The wise store up choice food and olive oil, but fools gulp theirs down."* By living within our means and saving for the future, we can avoid the dangers of debt and ensure a more secure financial future for ourselves and our families.

In conclusion, debt is a dangerous trap that can lead to financial and emotional distress. As Christians, we are called to be good stewards of the resources that God has given us, and to avoid debt. By living within our means, saving for the future, and avoiding the pitfalls of debt, we can achieve financial freedom and live a more fulfilling life.

The Biblical Approach To Debt

As Christians, we are called to be stewards of our finances and to use our resources in a way that honors God. One area that can often be a struggle for many of us is debt. In today's society, it is easy to accumulate debt, but the Bible has much to say about how we should handle it.

Foremost, we should seek to avoid debt. Proverbs 22:7 tells us that *"The rich rule over the poor, and the borrower is the slave of the lender."* When we borrow money, we are relinquishing control of our finances to someone else. Instead, we should strive to live within our means and avoid taking on debt that we cannot afford to repay.

However, there may be times when taking on debt is necessary, such as buying a home or pursuing higher education. In these cases, we should still strive to minimize our debt and be wise in our borrowing. Proverbs 21:5 tells us that "The plans of the diligent lead surely to abundance, but everyone who is hasty comes only to poverty." We should deliberate our options and make a plan to repay our debt as quickly as possible.

When we find ourselves in debt, we should prioritize paying it off. Romans 13:8 tells us to *"Owe no one anything, except to love each other."* Debt can be a burden that weighs us down and limits our ability to serve God and others. By paying off our debts, we can free ourselves to live more fully in God's calling.

Finally, we should approach debt with humility and seek help when we need it. Proverbs 15:22 tells us that *"Without counsel plans fail, but with many advisers they succeed."* If we are struggling with debt, we should seek the advice of trusted friends, family, or financial professionals. We should also be willing to make sacrifices and changes to our lifestyle in order to live within our means and honor God with our finances.

In summary, the biblical approach to debt is to avoid it, be wise in our borrowing, prioritize paying it off, and seek help when needed. By following these principles, we can be good stewards of the resources that God has entrusted to us and live more fully into His calling for our lives.

Practical Tips For Debt Management

Debt is a reality for many people, and it can be overwhelming and stressful. However, with a few practical tips, you can take control of your debt and improve your financial situation.

- **Create A Budget and Stick To It!**

The first step in managing your debt is to create a budget. This will help you see where your money is going and identify areas where you can cut back. Once you have a budget, stick to it. This will help you avoid overspending and keep your debt under control.

- **Prioritize Your Debt.**

If you have multiple debts, prioritize them based on interest rates and terms. Focus on paying off high-interest debts first, while making minimum payments on the rest. This will help you save money on interest in the long run.

- **Negotiate With Creditors.**

If you're struggling to make payments, don't be afraid to reach out to your creditors and negotiate a payment plan. Many creditors will work with you to come up with a plan that fits your budget.

- **Consider Consolidating Your Debt.**

If you have multiple debts with high interest rates, consolidating them into a single loan with a lower interest rate can help you save money on interest and simplify your payments.

- **Avoid New Debt.**

While you're working to pay off your existing debt, avoid taking on new debt. This means avoiding unnecessary purchases and using credit cards sparingly.

● **Seeking Support From Pros and Others.**

Managing debt can be challenging, but you don't have to do it alone. Consider seeking support from a financial advisor, credit counselor, or support group.

Remember, managing debt is a process, and it takes time and effort. But with these practical tips and a commitment to financial stewardship, you can take control of your debt and improve your financial situation.

Money and Giving in the Bible
The Biblical View On Giving

Giving is a fundamental aspect of Christian stewardship that is firmly rooted in the Bible. The Bible teaches us that giving is not only an expression of our love for God but also a way of participating in His work on earth. It is a demonstration of our faith and a way of acknowledging that everything we have comes from God.

The Bible teaches us that giving should be done willingly and cheerfully, expecting nothing in return. In 2 Corinthians 9:7, we read that *"Each of you should give what you have decided in your heart to give, not reluctantly or under compulsion, for God loves a cheerful giver."* This verse emphasizes the importance of giving from the heart, with no pressure or obligation.

Giving is not just about money; it also involves giving our time, talents, and resources to serve others. Jesus taught us that *"it is more blessed to give than to receive"* (Acts 20:35). As Christians, we are called to follow Jesus' example of selfless giving and sacrificial love. We are called to give generously and to use our resources to bless others.

One of the most well-known passages in the Bible about giving is found in Malachi 3:10, where God challenges His people to test Him in their giving. He says, *"Bring the whole tithe into the storehouse, that there may be food in my house. Test me in this,"* says the Lord Almighty, *"and see if I will not throw open the floodgates of heaven and pour out so much blessing that there will not be room enough to store it."*

Tithing, which is giving 10% of our income to the church, is a biblical principle that shows our obedience and faithfulness to God. It is a way of acknowledging that God is the source of our provisions and that we trust Him to provide for our needs.

Besides tithing, the Bible teaches us about giving to the poor. Proverbs 19:17 says, *"Whoever is kind to the poor lends to the Lord, and he will reward them for what they have done."* Giving to those in need is a way of showing compassion, mercy, and love, and it reflects our faith in God's provision.

Giving is an essential aspect of Christian stewardship, and it is a way of participating in God's work on earth. The Bible teaches us that giving should be done willingly and cheerfully, expecting nothing in return. We are called to give generously, using our time, talents, and resources to serve others, and to trust God to provide for our needs. Tithing and giving to the poor are biblical principles that show our obedience and faithfulness to God, and they are a way of expressing our love for Him and our gratitude for all that He has given us.

Examples Of Giving In The Bible

The Bible is filled with examples of giving, both in the Old and New Testaments. These examples illustrate the importance of generosity and stewardship in the lives of believers. Here are a few examples of giving in the Bible:

- **Abraham** - In Genesis 14, Abraham gave a tenth of everything he had to Melchizedek, the king of Salem and a priest of God. This act of giving showed Abraham's faith in God and his recognition God gave him everything he had.

- **Widow at Zarephath** - In 1 Kings 17, Elijah made himself a partaker in poverty with the women and her son. Her giving made her now a partaker in the blessing that abode on Elijah's life. God performed a creative miracle of supernatural provision that sustained the 3 of them throughout the famine.

- **The Widow's Mite** - In Mark 12, Jesus observed a poor widow giving two small copper coins to the temple treasury. While others were giving large amounts, Jesus said that the widow's small gift was worth more because she gave out of her poverty, while the others gave out of their abundance.

- **The Good Samaritan** - In Luke 10, Jesus tells the parable of the Good Samaritan, a man who showed mercy to a stranger in need. The Samaritan paid for the injured man's care and promised to pay any additional expenses. This act of giving showed the Samaritan's compassion and willingness to help those in need.

- **The Early Church** - In Acts 2 and 4, we read about the early Christian community sharing their possessions and resources with one another. They were united in heart and mind and willingly gave to those in need.

These examples of giving in the Bible teach us that giving is not just about money, but also about our time, talents, and resources. Giving should be done with a cheerful heart and a desire to serve others. As Christians, we are called to be good stewards of what God has given us and to use our resources to further His kingdom.

CODENAME: THE GIVER
Your Homework Assignment

The Bible is filled with examples of giving, both in the Old and New Testaments. These examples illustrate the importance of generosity and stewardship in the lives of believers.

Your assignment is to create a list of opportunities for giving in your family, neighborhood, your school, your work, your church and anywhere throughout your community that you can be a giver. Challenge yourself to list those opportunities below and then set a timeline or a date you will begin your weekly campaign of giving.

The Benefits Of Giving

As Christians, we are called to be generous with our resources and give to those in need. While giving may seem like a sacrifice, it actually comes with many benefits for both the giver and the receiver.

First, giving allows us to reflect God's character. The Bible tells us that God so loved the world that He gave His only Son (John 3:16). By giving to others, we show God's love to them and reflect His generosity. This act of giving also deepens our relationship with God and helps us to become more like Him.

Second, giving can bring us joy and satisfaction. Proverbs 11:25 says, *"A generous person will prosper; whoever refreshes others will be refreshed."* When we give to others, we experience a sense of happiness and fulfillment that cannot be found in material possessions.

Third, giving can have a positive impact on our finances. The Bible encourages us to give a portion of our income to the church or to those in need (Malachi 3:10, Luke 12:33). This act of giving can actually help us manage our money more effectively and avoid financial struggles.

Giving also is important for establishing community. We find in Luke 6:38 the most popular verse on giving. It reads, **"Give, and it shall be given unto you; good measure, pressed down, and shaken together, and running over, shall men give into your bosom. For with the same measure that ye mete withal it shall be measured to you again."** Meaning that your giving triggers a principle of reciprocity. God touches the hearts of men and women to show you favor. Doors of opportunity on your job, in the marketplace and in the ministry open up for you. Money and other resources make their way into your hands to steward over. Blessing upon blessing enters your life, so that God is honored through your life throughout your community.

Last, giving can have a ripple effect on our community and the world. When we give to others, we are not only meeting their immediate needs, but we are also inspiring others to give and creating a culture of generosity. This can lead to positive change and transformation in our communities and beyond.

In conclusion, giving is not just a commandment from God, but it is also a way to reflect His character, experience joy and satisfaction, improve our finances, and impact the world. As Christians, we are called to be faithful stewards of our resources and use them to bless others.

The Christian Perspective on Saving and Investing

The Importance Of Saving And Investing

The importance of saving and investing cannot be overstated in financial stewardship. As Christians, we are called to be wise with the resources God has given us, and that includes our money. Saving and investing are key components of financial planning and can help us achieve our long-term financial goals.

Saving is important because it allows us to build an emergency fund, which can help us weather unexpected financial storms. It also enables us to save for future expenses such as a down payment on a home or college tuition for our children. Saving also helps us avoid debt, as we are less likely to have to rely on credit cards or loans when we have money saved up.

Investing is important because it allows us to put our money to work for us. When we invest, we have the potential to earn a higher return than we would with a savings account or other low-risk investments. Of course, investing comes with risks, and it's important to do our research and seek professional advice before making any investment decisions.

As Christians, we should approach saving and investing with a biblical perspective. Proverbs 21:20 tells us, *"The wise store up choice food and olive oil, but fools gulp theirs down."* This verse encourages us to save and invest wisely, rather than spending all of our money on immediate pleasures.

We should also remember that our ultimate goal in saving and investing is not to accumulate wealth for ourselves, but to use our resources to further God's kingdom. Luke 12:33 says, *"Sell your possessions and give to the poor. Provide purses for yourselves that will not wear out, a treasure in heaven that will never fail, where no thief comes near and no moth destroys."* This verse reminds us that our earthly possessions are temporary, but our treasures in heaven are eternal.

Saving and investing are important components of financial stewardship. As Christians, we should approach these practices with a biblical perspective, seeking to use our resources to glorify God and further his kingdom. By being wise with our money, we can achieve our financial goals while also honoring God with our finances.

The Biblical Principles Of Saving And Investing

The Bible has a lot to say about saving and investing, and it is important for Christians to understand these principles in order to be good stewards of the financial resources that God has given them. Here are some of the key biblical principles of saving and investing:

- **START WITH A PLAN** - Proverbs 21:5 says, *"The plans of the diligent lead surely to abundance, but everyone who is hasty comes only to poverty."* It is important to have a plan for your finances, including a budget, savings goals, and investment strategies.

- **BE PATIENT** - Proverbs 13:11 says, *"Wealth gained hastily will dwindle, but whoever gathers little by little will increase it."* It takes time and patience to build wealth through saving and investing, so don't be tempted to take shortcuts or make risky investments.

- **DIVERSIFY YOUR INVESTMENTS** - Ecclesiastes 11:2 says, *"Divide your portion to seven, or even to eight, for you do not know what misfortune may occur on the earth."* This means that it is wise to spread your investments across different asset classes and industries, to reduce the risk of losing everything in a single investment.

- **AVOID DEBT** - Proverbs 22:7 says, *"The borrower is the slave of the lender."* Debt can be a major obstacle to saving and investing, so it is important to avoid taking on unnecessary debt and to pay off any existing debts as quickly as possible.

- **GIVE GENEROUSLY** - Proverbs 11:24-25 says, *"One gives freely, yet grows all the richer; another withholds what he should give and only suffers want. Whoever brings blessing will be enriched, and one who waters will himself be watered."* Giving generously not only pleases God, but it can also help to increase your wealth and financial blessings.

By following these biblical principles of saving and investing, Christians can be wise stewards of their financial resources and use them to further God's kingdom on earth. Remember, our ultimate goal should not be to accumulate wealth for its own sake, but to use our resources to bless others and bring glory to God.

Practical Tips For Saving And Investing

Saving and investing are two critical components of financial stewardship. Saving helps build a financial cushion that can weather unexpected expenses, and investing can help grow wealth over the long- term. Here are some practical tips for saving and investing:

- **Set Financial Goals:** With saving and investing, it's essential to have a clear idea of what you're trying to achieve. Set specific financial goals, such as saving for a down payment on a house, paying off debt, or building a retirement nest egg.

- **Create A Budget:** A budget is a powerful tool for managing your money. It helps you track your spending and identify areas where you can cut back to save more money. Be sure to include saving and investing as line items in your budget.

- **Start Small:** You don't need to have a lot of money to start saving and investing. Start small and escalate your contributions over time. Consistency is key in building wealth.

- **Take Advantage Of Employer-Sponsored Retirement Plan:** If your employer offers a retirement plan, such as a 401(k) or 403(b), be sure to take advantage of it. These plans offer tax benefits and can help you save for retirement.

- **Diversify Your Investments:** Don't put all your eggs in one basket. Diversify your investments by spreading your money across different asset classes, such as stocks, bonds, and real estate.

- **Avoid High Fees:** High fees can eat into your investment returns. Look for low-cost investment options, such as index funds and exchange-traded funds (ETFs).

- **Stay The Course:** Investing can be volatile, and it's easy to get caught up in short-term market fluctuations. Stay the course and stick to your long-term investment plan.

By following these practical tips, you can build a solid foundation for your financial future. Remember, financial stewardship is about more than just saving and investing. It's about using your resources wisely and in a way that honors God.

Biblical Wisdom On Budgeting & Financial Planning
The Importance Of Budgeting And Financial Planning

Budgeting and financial planning are crucial aspects of financial stewardship for Christians. The Bible teaches us the importance of managing our money wisely and being good stewards of the resources that God has blessed us with. In this subchapter, we will explore why budgeting and financial planning are essential for Christians and how we can apply biblical principles to manage our finances.

One of the primary reasons budgeting and financial planning are crucial for Christians is that they help us be good stewards of our money. As Christians, we are called to use our resources wisely and to glorify God with everything that we have. By creating a budget and financial plan, we can ensure that we are using our money in a way that honors God and helps us to achieve our financial goals.

Another reason budgeting and financial planning are important for Christians is that they help us avoid debt and financial stress. The Bible teaches us that debt is slavery (Proverbs 22:7) and that we should avoid it. By creating a budget and financial plan, we can ensure that we are living within our means and avoiding unnecessary debt.

Budgeting and financial planning also help us be more charitable. The Bible teaches us to be generous and to give to those in need (2 Corinthians 9:6-8). By managing our finances well, we can free up resources to give to others and to support ministries and organizations that are doing God's work.

In conclusion, budgeting and financial planning are essential aspects of financial stewardship for Christians. By managing our finances well, we can honor God, avoid debt and financial stress, and be more generous. Let us strive to be good stewards of the resources that God has blessed us with, and to use our finances in a way that brings glory to Him.

The Biblical Principles Of Budgeting And Financial Planning

Budgeting and financial planning are essential components of financial stewardship for Christians. The Bible provides several principles that guide believers in managing their finances. These principles not only help Christians to avoid financial struggles but also enable them to be charitable.

The second principle is to live within one's means. Christians should not spend more than they earn. This requires creating a budget that outlines all the expenses and allocating funds accordingly. Christians should also avoid debt and prioritize paying off any outstanding debts.

The first principle of budgeting and financial planning is to acknowledge that everything belongs to God. Christians are merely stewards of the resources that God has entrusted to them. Therefore, they need to use their finances in a way that honors God and aligns with His will. This means that Christians should prioritize giving to God's work through tithing and charitable giving.

The third principle is to save and invest wisely. The Bible encourages Christians to save for emergencies and the future. Investing in stocks, bonds, or real estate can also be a wise way to grow one's wealth. However, Christians should always seek guidance from God and practice discernment when making investment decisions.

The fourth principle is to be content with what one has. This means avoiding the temptation to compare oneself to others or to pursue material possessions for their own sake. Instead, Christians should focus on using their resources to glorify God and serve others.

Finally, budgeting and financial planning are critical components of Christian stewardship. By following these biblical principles, Christians can manage their finances in a way that honors God, avoids financial struggles, and enables generosity & charity.

Practical Tips For Budgeting And Financial Planning

Practical tips for budgeting and financial planning are essential for Christians who want to be good stewards of their money. The Bible teaches us to manage our finances wisely, and budgeting is a crucial tool in achieving financial stability and success. Here are some tips to help you budget and plan your finances effectively:

- **Create A Budget:** Start by listing all your sources of income and expenses. Categorize your expenses into essential and non-essential. Essential expenses include rent/mortgage, utilities, groceries, transportation, and healthcare. Non-essential expenses include entertainment, dining out, and shopping. Allocate a specific amount for each category and stick to it.

- **Save For Emergencies:** Set aside some money every month for unexpected expenses such as car repairs, medical bills, or job loss. Aim to have at least three to six months' worth of living expenses in an emergency fund.

- **Pay Off Debts:** If you have debts, prioritize paying them off as soon as possible. Start with the high-interest debts first, such as credit card debts or payday loans. Use the debt snowball method or debt avalanche method to pay off your debts faster.

- Plan For Retirement: Start saving for retirement as early as possible. Contribute to your employer's retirement plan, such as a 401(k), if available. If not, consider opening an IRA or Roth IRA. Aim to save at least 15% of your income for retirement.

- Give Generously: The Bible teaches us to give generously to those in need. Allocate a portion of your income for charitable giving. Consider supporting your church, missions, or organizations that serve the needy.

● Review your budget regularly: Review your budget regularly to ensure that you are staying on track. Make adjustments as necessary to reflect changes in your income or expenses.

In conclusion, budgeting and financial planning are crucial for Christians who want to honor God with their finances. By following these practical tips, you can achieve financial stability, pay off debts, save for emergencies and retirement, and give generously to those in need. Remember, everything we have belongs to God, and we are called to be faithful stewards of His resources.

The Role Of Tithing In Christian Stewardship
The Biblical Perspective On Tithing

The biblical perspective on tithing is an essential topic that every Christian should understand in their journey towards financial stewardship. Tithing is not just a financial practice but also a spiritual discipline that reflects our obedience and gratitude to God. In this subchapter, we will explore the biblical teachings on tithing and its significance in Christian stewardship.

The word "tithe" means a tenth. In the Old Testament, tithing was a requirement for the Israelites to give a tenth of their income to support the Levites and priests who served in the temple (Leviticus 27:30, Numbers 18:21-28). Tithing was also a way for them to show their trust in God's provision and acknowledge that everything they had came from Him.

In the New Testament, Jesus affirmed the practice of tithing (Matthew 23:23) and even went further to emphasize the importance of giving generously and sacrificially (Mark 12:41-44, Luke 21:1-4). Paul also encouraged the early Christians to give generously and cheerfully (2 Corinthians 9:6-8).

Tithing is not just an obligation but also a privilege and an act of worship. When we give our tithes and offerings, we acknowledge God's sovereignty over our finances and express our faith in His provision. Tithing also helps us to prioritize our finances and put God first in our lives (Proverbs 3:9-10).

However, tithing is not a magic formula for financial prosperity. It reflects our heart and our relationship with God. We should not give out of compulsion or guilt, but out of love and gratitude for what God has done for us. Giving should also be done in secret, without seeking recognition or praise from others (Matthew 6:1-4).

Tithing is an essential aspect of Christian stewardship that reflects our trust in God's provision and our obedience to His commands. We should give generously and cheerfully, not out of obligation or fear, but out of love and gratitude for what God has done for us. Let us strive to be faithful stewards of God's resources, including our finances, and use them for His glory and the advancement of His kingdom.

The Importance Of Tithing

Tithing was a common practice in Jewish culture. Tithing is also one of the most important aspects of Christian stewardship. It is a practice that God's people have observed since ancient times, and it is a powerful way to demonstrate our faith and trust in Him. Tithing is not just a financial obligation, but a spiritual act of worship that reflects our love and commitment to God.

The word "tithe" means "tenth." In the Old Testament, God commanded His people to give a tenth of their income to support the work of the temple and the priests. The purpose of this practice was to provide for the needs of the community and to honor God with the first fruits of their labor.

Tithing is a way to acknowledge that everything we have ultimately comes from God and to support the work of the church and other ministries.

To me, the most important theme or example of tithing comes from the book of Genesis chapters 14 & 15. In these portions of scripture Abram, later known as Abraham, gives a tithe to the king of Salem, Melchizedek. Melchizedek is referred to as "the priest of God Most High." in verse 18 of Genesis chapter 14. He is the first example of what is referred to in 1 Peter 2:9 as, "a royal priesthood"; both king and priest at once. Anointed to serve and lead the people of his nation, but also chosen as God's servant to his people. The dual role places a unique responsibility on Melchizedek and those that follow. Including King David, King Jesus and You. It is a powerful opportunity to hear from God, gain instructions and wisdom for leading His people and representing Him as a royal priest, an ambassador, a witness to His Grace, Mercy and Salvation.

Abram gave a tithe, or one-tenth, of all his possessions to King Melchizedek. In this chapter the tithe is also representative as an oath unto God. Abram is determined to make sure that God gets all the glory for his prosperity. He states in Genesis 14:22 & 23, *"I have raised my hand and sworn an oath to the Lord God Most High, the Creator and Possessor of heaven and earth, that I would not take anything that is yours, from a thread to a sandal strap, so you could not say, 'I [the King of Sodom] have made Abram rich."*

The story does not end there. God responds to Abram honoring his vow in verse 1 of chapter 15 of Genesis, *"After these things the word of the Lord came to Abram in a vision, saying, "Do not be afraid, Abram, I am your shield; Your reward [for obedience] shall be very great."* Tithing is not charity but an act of obedience and honor in the sight of God. Let yourself be found faithful and obedient in His Eyes.

In the New Testament, Jesus affirmed the importance of tithing and encouraged His followers to give generously to support the work of the church and to care for the needs of the poor.

Tithing is not just about money, but about faith. When we give a tenth of our income to God, everything we have comes from Him and belongs to Him. Tithing is a way to show our trust in God's provision and to show our gratitude for His blessings. It is also a way to put God first in our lives and to prioritize His kingdom above our own desires and needs.

Tithing is also a way to take part in the church's work and to support the ministry of God's people. The church needs resources to carry out its mission of spreading the gospel, caring for the needs of the community, and making disciples. Tithing is a way to contribute to this important work and to partner with God in His mission.

Finally, tithing is a way to experience God's blessings and provision in our lives. When we give generously and sacrificially, God promises to bless us and to provide for our needs. Tithing is not a way to earn God's favor or to manipulate Him, but a way to trust in His faithfulness and to experience His grace.

In conclusion, tithing is a vital part of Christian stewardship. It is a way to show our faith, to support the work of the church, and to experience God's blessings. As we give generously and sacrificially, we honor God with our resources and take part in His mission to redeem the world.

Practical Tips For Tithing

Tithing is an essential part of Christian stewardship. It involves giving one-tenth of our income to God as an act of worship and obedience. While tithing is a biblical mandate, it's challenging to implement practically. Here are some practical tips for tithing:

- **Make Tithing A Priority:** Tithing should be the first thing you do when you receive your income. Set aside 10% of your income before paying bills, buying groceries, or making any other expenses. This will ensure that you honor God with your first fruits and put Him first in your finances.

- **Use A Budget:** A budget is an essential tool for managing your finances, including tithing. Allocate 10% of your income to tithing in your budget and stick to it. Having a budget will help you track your expenses and ensure that you do not overspend and fail to tithe.

- **Give Cheerfully:** Tithing should be a joyful act of worship, not a burden. Give with a cheerful heart, knowing that you are honoring God and contributing to His work on earth. Do not give grudgingly or out of compulsion.

- **Give Consistently:** Tithing should be a regular practice, not a onetime event. Make it a habit to tithe every time you receive your income, whether it is weekly, bi-weekly, or monthly. Consistency will help you develop discipline and honor God consistently.

- **Give Sacrificially:** While tithing involves giving 10% of your income, you can also give more if you feel led by the Holy Spirit. Giving sacrificially means giving beyond your comfort zone and trusting God to provide for your needs. It is an act of faith that shows your trust in God's provision.

Tithing should be a practical expression of our faith and obedience to God. By making it a priority, using a budget, giving cheerfully and consistently, and giving sacrificially, we honor God with our finances and contribute to His work on earth.

Biblical Teachings On Generosity & Charitable Giving

The Biblical View On Generosity

The biblical view on generosity is a crucial aspect of financial stewardship for Christians. The Bible teaches that generosity is not just a good deed but a commandment that Christians must follow. God, through His Word, encourages Christians to be generous with their time, talents, and treasures. Generosity is a vital part of Christian life and an essential aspect of financial stewardship.

The Bible teaches God is a generous giver. He gave His only Son, Jesus Christ, to save humanity from sin and death. In 2 Corinthians 9:7, Paul writes, *"Each one must give as he has decided in his heart, not reluctantly or under compulsion, for God loves a cheerful giver."* This verse highlights the importance of giving willingly and generously, without being forced or pressured.

Generosity is not just about giving money. Christians can be generous by sharing their time, talents, and resources with those in need. In Luke 6:38, Jesus says, *"Give, and it will be given to you. Good measure, pressed down, shaken together, running over, will be put into your lap. For with the measure you use, it will be measured back to you."* This verse emphasizes the reward of generosity and the blessing that comes with giving.

The Bible also teaches that generosity should be done without seeking recognition or praise. In Matthew 6:1-4, Jesus says, "Beware of practicing your righteousness before other people in order to be seen by them, for then you will have no reward from your Father who is in heaven. Thus, when you give to the needy, sound no trumpet before you, as the hypocrites do in the synagogues and in the streets, that they may be praised by others. Truly, I say to you, they have received their reward. But when you give to the needy, do not let your left hand know what your right hand is doing, so that your giving may be in secret. And your Father who sees in secret will reward you."

In conclusion, the biblical view on generosity is clear. Christians are called to be generous with their time, talents, and treasures. Generosity is not just a good deed but a commandment that Christians must follow. It is essential to give willingly and generously without seeking recognition or praise. By doing so, we become a channel of blessings to others, and God blesses us in return.

Examples Of Generosity In The Bible

The Bible is full of examples of generosity, and God wants His people to be generous with their possessions and resources. From the Old Testament to the New Testament, the Bible is filled with stories of people who gave generously and were blessed because of it.

One of the most famous examples of generosity in the Bible is the story of the widow's mite. In Mark 12:41-44, Jesus and His disciples are in the temple watching people put their offerings into the treasury. Many rich people put in large amounts, but a poor widow put in two small copper coins, worth only a few cents. Jesus pointed out to His disciples that the widow gave more than all the others because she gave all she had.

Another example of generosity in the Bible is found in the Old Testament story of the widow of Zarephath. In 1 Kings 17:7-16, Elijah the prophet came to the widow's home and asked her for a drink of water and a piece of bread. The widow told Elijah that she only had enough flour and oil left to make one small cake of bread for herself and her son, and then they would surely die.

But Elijah told her to make him a cake first and promised that her flour and oil would not run out until the drought was over. The widow trusted God's promise, and her flour and oil never ran out.

In the New Testament, we also see examples of generosity among the early Christians. In Acts 4:32-37, we read the believers were of one heart and mind, and no one claimed that any of their possessions was their own.

Instead, they shared everything they had, and those who had land or houses sold them and brought the money to the apostles to be distributed to those in need.

These examples of generosity in the Bible show us that God wants us to be generous with our possessions and resources. When we give generously, we show our trust in God and our willingness to be good stewards of the blessings He has given us. May we all strive to be like the generous men and women of the Bible, and may our generosity bring glory to God and blessings to others.

The Benefits Of Generosity

The Bible is filled with teachings on the importance of generosity and charitable giving. As Christians, we are called to be generous with our resources, time, and talents. The benefits of living a generous life are not just limited to the recipients of our giving, but they also have a positive impact on our own lives.

One benefit of generosity is that it allows us to experience the joy of giving. When we give, we can make a difference in the lives of others and help them in their time of need. This brings a sense of satisfaction and fulfillment that cannot be found through material possessions.

Generosity also helps to cultivate a spirit of gratitude and contentment. When we focus on giving to others, we become less focused on our own wants and desires. This can help us appreciate what we have and to be content with what we have been blessed with.

Generosity has been shown to have physical and emotional health benefits. Studies have found that people who give regularly have lower levels of stress and depression. Giving has also been linked to lower blood pressure, increased happiness, and longer life expectancy.

Besides these personal benefits, generosity also has a positive impact on our communities and the world. When we give to charitable organizations, we can support programs that help those in need, such as feeding the hungry, providing shelter for the homeless, and caring for the sick. Our generosity can also inspire others to give, creating a ripple effect of kindness and compassion.

Overall, generosity is an essential part of living a Christian life. By giving generously, we have the opportunity to make a difference in the lives of others, cultivate gratitude and contentment in our own lives, and promote a spirit of kindness and compassion in our communities. As we seek to be good stewards of the resources God has given us, let us strive to live lives of generosity and service to others.

The Connection Between Your Faith & Your Finances

The Relationship Between Faith And Finances In The Bible

The relationship between faith and finances is a topic that may seem paradoxical, but it is an essential aspect of Christian stewardship. The Bible has much to say about how we should handle our finances and material possessions, and it all begins with faith. Our faith in God should be the foundation of our financial decisions, and our financial decisions should reflect our faith in God.

One of the most significant ways that faith and finances are connected is through tithing. Tithing is the act of giving a portion of our income to the church or to those in need. The Bible teaches us that tithing is an act of obedience and a way to honor God with our finances. It expresses our faith in God's provision and our willingness to trust Him with our finances.

Another way faith and finances are connected is through our attitudes towards money. The Bible teaches us that money is not evil, but the love of money can be. We are warned against the dangers of greed and materialism, and we are called to be content with what we have. Our faith should shape our perspective on money, and we should strive to use our finances in a way that honors God.

The Bible also teaches us about the importance of work and earning a living. We are called to be diligent in our work and to provide for our families. Our faith should motivate us to work hard and use our talents and abilities to glorify God. We should also be wise in our financial planning and budgeting, recognizing that everything we have belongs to God.

One of the most significant ways our faith and finances are connected is through generosity and charitable giving. The Bible teaches us we are blessed to be a blessing, and we are called to share our resources with those in need. Our faith should inspire us to give generously and to use our finances to make a positive impact in the world.

In conclusion, the relationship between faith and finances is a crucial aspect of Christian stewardship. Our faith should be the foundation of our financial decisions, and our financial decisions should reflect our faith in God. Tithing, attitudes towards money, work, financial planning, and charitable giving are all areas where our faith and finances intersect. As Christians, we are called to be faithful stewards of all that God has entrusted to us, including our finances and material possessions.

The Biblical Principles Of Faith And Finances

The biblical principles of faith and finances are foundational to understanding the role of money in the life of a Christian. Money is a tool that can be used to further God's kingdom and bless others, but it can also be a stumbling block that leads to greed, materialism, and financial struggles. In this chapter, we will explore several key biblical principles that can guide our approach to finances and help us become faithful stewards of the resources God has given us.

Foremost, the Bible teaches us that all things belong to God (Psalm 24:1). This includes our money and possessions. As stewards, we are called to manage these resources wisely and with a mindset of generosity. This means recognizing that everything we have is a gift from God and using it in ways that honor Him.

One of the key principles of financial stewardship in the Bible is debt management. God warns us about the dangers of debt and encourages us to live within our means (Proverbs 22:7). This means avoiding excessive debt and making wise choices about borrowing and lending. We are called to be faithful in paying our debts and to avoid becoming enslaved to financial obligations.

Another important principle is the role of giving in the Bible. God calls us to be generous and to give cheerfully to those in need (2 Corinthians 9:7).

Whether through tithing or charitable giving, we are called to be good stewards of our resources and to use them to bless others. Giving is an act of faith that shows our trust in God's provision and our willingness to put His priorities above our own.

The Bible also teaches us about saving and investing. While we are not to trust in wealth or material possessions, we are called to be wise stewards of what we have been given. This means setting aside money for emergencies, planning for the future, and investing in opportunities that align with our values and priorities.

Finally, the Bible teaches us about the connection between faith and finances. Our attitude toward money reflects our relationship with God and our trust in His provision. When we approach finances with a mindset of faith and obedience, we can experience the peace and joy that comes from living in alignment with God's will.

In conclusion, the biblical principles of faith and finances provide a solid foundation for financial stewardship. By following these principles, we can become faithful stewards of the resources God has given us and use them to bless others and further His kingdom.

Practical Tips For Integrating Faith And Finances

Practical tips for integrating faith and finances can help Christians become better stewards of their finances. One of the first steps in integrating faith and finances is to pray for wisdom and guidance. God is the ultimate provider, and we can trust Him to guide us in our financial decisions. Here are some other practical tips to consider:

- **Create A Budget Based On Biblical Principles.** A budget is a tool that can help us manage our finances better. It is essential to create a budget that is based on biblical principles, such as prioritizing giving, avoiding debt, and living within our means.

- **Be Content With What You Have:** I want to emphasize how important this principle is to sustained spiritual growth. The Bible teaches us to be content with what we have and not to covet what others have. It is essential to avoid the trap of consumerism and to focus on the things that truly matter in life.

- **Practice Generosity And Charitable Giving:** The Bible teaches us to be generous and to give to those in need. We can honor God by giving to our church, supporting missionaries, and helping those who are less fortunate.

- **Seek Wise Counsel:** Seek the advice of trusted Christian financial advisors or mentors who can offer guidance and accountability in managing your finances.

- **Avoid Debt:** The Bible warns us about the dangers of debt and encourages us to live within our means. Avoiding debt can help us avoid unnecessary stress and financial burdens.

• **Save For The Future:** It is important to save for the future and to plan for unexpected expenses. We can honor God by being good stewards of the resources He has entrusted to us.

• **Remember That Work Is A Gift From God:** The Bible teaches us that work is a gift from God and that we should work with excellence and diligence. We can honor God by doing our best in our work and using our resources to bless others.

Integrating faith and finances is a lifelong journey that involves seeking God's guidance, practicing biblical principles, and being accountable to others. By following these practical tips, Christians can become better stewards of their finances and honor God with their resources.

Biblical Advice On Overcoming Financial Struggles

The Common Financial Struggles Christians Face

As Christians, we strive to live our lives under the teachings of the Bible. However, with our finances, we often struggle to align our beliefs with our actions. The Bible has much to say about financial stewardship, but many Christians face common financial struggles that can hinder their ability to manage their finances biblically.

One of the most common financial struggles faced by Christians is debt. In today's society, it is easy to succumb to the temptation to borrow money for everything from a new car to a big-screen TV. However, the Bible teaches we should avoid debt and that we should work to pay off any debts we incur as quickly as possible.

Another common struggle faced by Christians is the challenge of balancing our desire to give generously with our need to provide for ourselves and our families. The Bible teaches we should be generous with our resources, but it also emphasizes the importance of responsible stewardship. Finding a balance between these two competing priorities can be difficult, but it is essential to living a financially healthy and biblically grounded life.

Besides these challenges, Christians may also struggle with issues such as overspending, lack of financial discipline, and difficulty saving for the future. These struggles can be overcome through a combination of biblical wisdom, practical advice, and a commitment to living under the teachings of the Bible.

Ultimately, the key to overcoming these financial struggles is to remember that our resources are not our own, but are instead gifts from God. As we seek to manage our finances in a way that honors Him, we find that our financial struggles are transformed into opportunities for growth, generosity, and faithfully steward over all that God has entrusted to us.

The Biblical Approach To Overcoming Financial Struggles

The Bible offers a wealth of wisdom for Christians who are struggling with financial difficulties. These timeless principles can help believers to overcome their financial struggles and achieve financial freedom.

One of the key principles of biblical financial stewardship is the importance of living within one's means. The Bible teaches we should not be in debt to anyone, except for the debt of love (Romans 13:8). This means that we should avoid taking on unnecessary debt, and work to pay off any debts that we have as quickly as possible.

Another important principle is the importance of giving. The Bible teaches we should give generously and cheerfully, expecting nothing in return (2 Corinthians 9:6-7). This means that we should give to those in need, whether it be through tithes and offerings at church, or through charitable giving to organizations that are doing good work in our communities.

The Bible also teaches us to be wise stewards of our money, and to plan for the future. This means that we should be diligent in our work and save money for emergencies and future needs (Proverbs 21:5). We should also be careful not to be greedy or covetous, but to be content with what we have (Hebrews 13:5).

If you are struggling with financial difficulties, the first step is to seek God's guidance and wisdom. Spend time in prayer and reflection, asking God to show you the areas where you need to change your financial life. Seek the advice of trusted friends and family members, and consider working with a financial advisor or credit counselor to help you get back on track.

Remember that God is faithful, and that He promises to provide for all our needs (Philippians 4:19). By following the biblical principles of financial stewardship, you can overcome your financial struggles and experience the joy and freedom of living a debt-free and financially secure life.

Practical Tips For Overcoming Financial Struggles

Financial struggles are a common issue that many people face in their lives. It could be because of various reasons such as job loss, unexpected expenses, debts, or poor financial management. However, as Christians, we have access to God's guidance and wisdom through the Bible to help us overcome these struggles. Here are some practical tips for overcoming financial struggles:

- **Seek God's Wisdom:** The Bible is full of wisdom on how to manage finances. Reading and meditating on scriptures such as Proverbs 13:11, Proverbs 22:7, and Matthew 6:19-21. Pray and ask God for guidance on how to manage your finances.

- **Create A Budget:** A budget is a tool that helps you track your income and expenses. It allows you to see where your money is going and identify areas where you can cut back. Create a realistic budget and stick to it. Consider using apps or software to help you track your budget.

- **Prioritize Your Expenses:** When you're struggling financially, it's essential to prioritize your expenses. Focus on paying for necessities such as food, shelter, and utilities before spending money on luxuries. Consider cutting back on non-essential expenses such as eating out or subscription services.

- **Increase Your Income:** Look for ways to increase your income, such as taking on a part-time job, selling items you no longer need, or starting a side business. Consider using your skills or talents to generate income.

- **Seek Support:** Don't be afraid to seek support from your family, friends, or a financial counselor. They can offer advice, guidance, and support as you navigate your financial struggles.

- **Stay Motivated:** Overcoming financial struggles can be challenging, but it's essential to stay motivated. Celebrate minor victories, such as paying off a debt or sticking to your budget. Keep reminding yourself of your financial goals and the benefits of financial freedom.

In conclusion, overcoming financial struggles requires discipline, determination, and faith. By following these practical tips and seeking God's guidance, you can overcome your financial struggles and achieve financial freedom. Remember, as Christians, we are called to be good stewards of our finances, and with God's help, we can manage our money wisely.

The Significance Of Work And Earning In The Bible

The Biblical View On Work And Earning

The biblical view on work and earning is an essential topic for Christians to understand in financial stewardship. The Bible has much to say about work and earning, and it is crucial to understand what it teaches on the subject.

First, the Bible teaches that work is good. In Genesis, we see God worked to create the world, and He created humans to work and take care of it. In Colossians 3:23-24, we read, *"Whatever you do, work at it with all your heart, as working for the Lord, not for human masters, since you know you will receive an inheritance from the Lord as a reward. It is the Lord Christ you are serving."* This passage reminds us that our work is not just for our bosses or for money, but ultimately for the Lord.

The Bible teaches we should earn our living through honest work. In 2 Thessalonians 3:10, we read, *"For even when we were with you, we gave you this rule: 'The one who is unwilling to work shall not eat.'"* This verse emphasizes the importance of working for our food and livelihood instead of relying on handouts or dishonest means of making money.

However, the Bible also warns against the love of money and pursuing wealth as an ultimate goal. In 1 Timothy 6:10, we read, "For the love of money is a root of all kinds of evil. Some people, eager for money, have wandered from the faith and pierced themselves with many griefs." This verse reminds us that our pursuit of wealth should not take priority over our faith and relationship with God.

The Bible teaches our earnings should be used for good and to bless others. In 2 Corinthians 9:7, we read, *"Each of you should give what you have decided in your heart to give, not reluctantly or under compulsion, for God loves a cheerful giver."* This verse reminds us that our earnings should not only be used for our own needs but also to help others.

In conclusion, the biblical view on work and earning emphasizes the importance of honest work, the avoidance of a love of money, and the use of our earnings to bless others. As Christians, we should strive to apply these principles to our financial stewardship and seek to honor God in all aspects of our lives, including our work and earning.

Examples Of Work And Earning In The Bible

The Bible has countless examples of work and earning that provide guidance on how Christians can manage their finances. One of the most well-known examples is that of Joseph, who began as a slave and eventually rose to become the second-in-command in Egypt, managing the country's economy during a severe famine. Joseph's wisdom, hard work, and faithfulness to God led to his success.

Another example is that of Ruth, who worked hard gleaning in the fields to provide for herself and her mother-in-law. Through her hard work and dedication, Ruth caught the eye of Boaz, a wealthy landowner who eventually became her husband. Another example of a woman who found success through hard work is Ruth. After the death of her husband, Ruth left her homeland of Moab and traveled to Bethlehem with her mother-in-law, Naomi. In Bethlehem, Ruth worked hard gleaning in the fields to provide for herself and Naomi. Her hard work and dedication eventually caught the eye of Boaz, a wealthy landowner who eventually became her husband.

Ruth's story is a powerful example of how hard work and dedication can lead to success. Ruth was not afraid to work hard, even in difficult circumstances. She was also willing to put the needs of others before her own, as she did for Naomi. Ruth's story is a reminder that anyone can achieve success, regardless of their circumstances, if they will work hard and never give up.

In the New Testament, the apostle Paul is a prime example of someone who worked hard to earn a living. He was a tentmaker by trade and often supported himself financially while preaching the gospel. Paul also taught the importance of hard work and earning a living in his letters to the churches.

In the New Testament, the apostle Paul was a prime example of a hard worker. He was a tentmaker by trade and often supported himself financially while preaching the gospel. Paul also taught the importance of hard work and earning a living in his letters to the churches.

In his letter to the Thessalonians, Paul wrote, "If anyone is not willing to work, let him not eat" (2 Thessalonians 3:10). This verse emphasizes the importance of self-sufficiency and the responsibility of each individual to provide for their own needs. Paul also encouraged Christians to work hard and to be diligent in their labors, writing, "Whatever you do, do it heartily, as to the Lord and not to men" (Colossians 3:23).

Paul's teachings on hard work and earning a living were rooted in his belief that all Christians are called to be productive members of society. He saw work as a way to glorify God and to serve others. He also believed that work could be a source of joy and satisfaction.

Paul's example and teachings on hard work are a valuable reminder for Christians today. In a world that is increasingly focused on materialism and instant gratification, it is important to remember the importance of hard work and self-sufficiency. Paul's teachings can help us live lives that are both productive and fulfilling.

Jesus also spoke about work and earning in several parables, such as the parable of the talents. In this story, a master gives his servants different amounts of money and expects them to use it wisely and increase it. The servants who worked hard and earned a profit were praised, while the one who buried his money was condemned.

Jesus also talked about work and earning in a few parables, like the parable of the talents. In this story, a master gives his servants different amounts of money and expects them to use it wisely and increase it. The servants who worked hard and made a profit were praised, while the one who buried his money was condemned.

The parable of the talents is a reminder that we're called to use our gifts and talents to glorify God and make a difference in the world. When we bury our talents, we're not only failing to fulfill our potential, but we're also depriving the world of the good we could accomplish.

The parable of the talents also teaches us the importance of hard work and perseverance. The master praised the servants who worked hard and made a profit, while the one who buried his money was condemned. This shows us that God rewards those who are diligent and who will put in the effort to succeed.

The parable of the talents reminds us we're accountable to God for how we use our resources. The master in the story expected his servants to use the money he had given them wisely. If they had not done so, he would have been displeased with them. In the same way, God expects us to use our resources wisely and to make the most of the opportunities that He has given us.

The parable of the talents is a valuable lesson for all of us. It reminds us of our responsibility to use our gifts and talents to glorify God, to make a difference in the world, and to be good stewards of the resources that He has given us.

Overall, the Bible teaches that work and earning are important aspects of financial stewardship. Christians are called to work hard and use their skills and abilities to provide for themselves and their families. However, it's important to remember that our ultimate trust and security should be in God and not in our wealth or possessions. As Proverbs 23:4-5 says, *"Do not wear yourself out to get rich; do not trust your own cleverness. Cast but a glance at riches, and they are gone, for they will surely sprout wings and fly off to the sky like an eagle."*

In conclusion, the Bible provides many examples of work and earning that can guide Christians in their financial stewardship. By working hard, managing their finances wisely, and trusting in God, Christians can honor Him with their wealth and resources.

The Benefits Of Work And Earning

In the Bible, work and earning are celebrated as blessings from God. Work is not a punishment, but a means of fulfilling God's purpose for our lives.

Earning is not just about financial wealth, but about the satisfaction and fulfillment that come from doing something meaningful. In this subchapter, we will explore the various benefits of work and earning that are highlighted in the Bible.

First, work and earning provide us with a sense of purpose and direction. God created us with unique talents and abilities that are used for His glory. When we engage in work that aligns with our passions and abilities, we experience a sense of fulfillment and purpose. In addition, earning provides us with the means to support ourselves and our families, as well as to give generously to others.

Second, work and earning cultivate discipline and responsibility. In order to succeed in our work, we must learn to manage our time, resources, and relationships wisely. We are also called to be good stewards of the financial blessings that come our way. This means being responsible for our spending, investing, and giving.

Third, work and earning build character and resilience. The Bible teaches us we will face challenges and difficulties in life, but that we can overcome them through faith and perseverance. By working hard and earning our way, we develop a strong work ethic, resilience, and perseverance that can carry us through life's challenges.

Finally, work and earning provide us with opportunities to serve others and make a positive impact in the world. Whether we are working in a paid or volunteer capacity, we can use our skills and resources to bless others and make a difference in their lives.

The Bible teaches us we are called to love our neighbors as ourselves, and that one way to do this is by serving them through our work and giving.

In conclusion, work and earning are not just about financial wealth, but about fulfilling God's purpose for our lives, cultivating discipline and responsibility, building character and resilience, and serving others. As Christians, we are called to be good stewards of the blessings that God has given us, including our work and earning potential. By embracing these blessings and using them for God's glory, we can experience the fullness and abundance of life that He has promised us.

A Christian's Guide To Managing Wealth And Material Possessions

The Biblical Perspective On Wealth And Material Possessions

The biblical perspective on wealth and material possessions is a topic that has been widely debated among Christians. While some believe that wealth is a blessing from God, others see it as a potential source of temptation and distraction from our spiritual life. However, what does the Bible really say about wealth and material possessions?

The Bible has a lot to say about wealth and material possessions. The teachings are complex and multifaceted, and it's important to consider all of them in order to get a complete picture.

Some of the most common themes that emerge from the Bible's teachings on wealth and possessions include:

- **The importance of stewardship.** God has given us all our possessions, and we are responsible for using them wisely. This means using them to glorify God, to help others, and to meet our own needs.

- **The dangers of materialism.** When we become too focused on material possessions, we can lose sight of what is truly important in life. This can lead to greed, selfishness, and other sins.

- **The blessing of giving.** God loves a cheerful giver, and when we give to others, we are not only blessing them, but we are also blessing ourselves.

It's important to remember that the Bible does not condemn wealth. In fact, there are many examples of wealthy people who were used by God to do great things. However, the Bible warns us against the dangers of materialism and the temptation to put our trust in our possessions.

Ultimately, the Bible's teachings on wealth and possessions are about our relationship with God. When we put our trust in God and use our possessions to glorify Him, we will find true happiness and fulfillment.

The Bible acknowledges the importance of wealth and material possessions in our lives. In 1 Timothy 6:17-19, Paul writes, *"Command those who are rich in this present world not to be arrogant nor to put their hope in wealth, which is so uncertain, but to put their hope in God, who richly provides us with everything for our enjoyment. Command them to do good, to be rich in good deeds, in generosity and charity. In this way, they will lay up treasure for themselves as a firm foundation for the coming age, so that they may take hold of the life that is truly life."*

From this passage, we can see that wealth and material possessions are not inherently evil, but it is our attitude towards them that matters. We are called to use our wealth to do good, be generous, and share with others. Our focus should not be on accumulating more wealth, but on using what we have been given to help those in need.

The Bible warns us about the dangers of greed and the love of money. In Matthew 6:24, Jesus says, *"No one can serve two masters. Either you will hate the one and love the other, or you will be devoted to the one and despise the other. You cannot serve both God and money."* We must be careful not to let our desire for wealth and possessions consume us, as it can lead us away from God.

The Bible teaches us about the importance of contentment. In Philippians 4:11-12, Paul writes, *"I have learned to be content whatever the circumstances. I know what it is to be in need, and I know what it is to have plenty. I have learned the secret of being content in any and every situation, whether well fed or hungry, whether living in plenty or in want."* As Christians, we should strive to be content with what we have and not constantly strive for more.

In conclusion, the Bible does not condemn wealth and material possessions, but it warns us of the dangers of greed and the love of money. As Christians, we are called to use our wealth to do good, be generous, and share with others, while also being content with what we have. Our focus should always be on serving God, rather than serving money.

The Christian's Responsibility As A Manager Of Wealth And Material Possessions

As Christians, we are called to be good stewards of the resources that God has given us, including our wealth and material possessions. While it's easy to become consumed by the desire for more money, bigger houses, and fancier cars, it is important to remember that these things are temporary and fleeting. Instead, we should focus on using our resources to glorify God and further His kingdom.

One of the most important aspects of financial stewardship is the concept of giving. Throughout the Bible, we see examples of generosity and charitable giving, from the widow who gave her last two coins to the church to the Good Samaritan who gave of his time and resources to help a stranger in need. As Christians, we are called to follow in these footsteps, giving generously and sacrificially to those in need and to the work of the church.

However, giving is only one aspect of financial stewardship. We are also called to manage our wealth and material possessions wisely, using them to further God's kingdom and provide for our families. This means avoiding debt living within our means, and being mindful of our spending habits. It also means investing wisely and saving for the future, so that we can provide for ourselves and our loved ones in times of need.

Of course, managing our wealth and material possessions also involves recognizing that these things are not the most important aspects of our lives. We should always put our relationship with God foremost, recognizing that our wealth and possessions are gifts from Him and should be used to further His kingdom, not our own desires.

Ultimately, the Christian's responsibility as a manager of wealth and material possessions is to use these resources wisely and in a way that honors God. By being mindful of our spending habits, investing wisely, and giving sacrificially, we can be good stewards of the resources that God has given us and further His kingdom.

Practical Tips For Managing Wealth And Material Possessions

Managing wealth and material possessions can be a daunting task, but as Christians, we are called to be good stewards of the resources God has given us. The Bible provides practical tips for managing our finances and possessions, and here are some of them:

Create A Budget: The Bible encourages us to plan and be responsible for our resources. Creating a budget will help you track your income and expenses and make informed financial decisions.

Avoid Debt: The Bible teaches us that borrowing money can lead to slavery and financial ruin. While some forms of debt may be necessary, it is important to avoid excessive borrowing and prioritize paying off debts.

Give Generously: Giving is an act of worship and obedience to God. The Bible encourages us to be generous with our resources and to give out of a cheerful heart.

Save And Invest Wisely: The Bible teaches us to be diligent and wise with our resources. Saving and investing can help us prepare for the future and provide for our families.

Avoid Materialism: The Bible warns us against the dangers of materialism and the love of money. We should focus on the eternal rather than the temporal and prioritize our relationship with God over our possessions.

Seek Wise Counsel: The Bible encourages us to seek wise counsel and surround ourselves with people who will give us sound financial advice. We should also be open to learning and growing in our understanding of financial stewardship.

Honor God With Your Work: The Bible teaches us that work is a gift from God, and we should honor Him by working diligently and with integrity. We should also use our skills and resources to serve others and advance His kingdom.

Managing wealth and material possessions is an important aspect of Christian stewardship. By following these practical tips and seeking guidance from the Bible, we can honor God with our finances and live a life of generosity, wisdom, and faithfulness.

Conclusion

Summary Of Key Points

In this book, "God's Master Plan For Money: A Biblical Guide to Financial Stewardship," we have explored various aspects of financial stewardship from a biblical perspective. The Bible has much to say about money and how we should manage it as Christians. Here are some of the key points we have covered in this book:

- Financial stewardship is a Christian responsibility - As Christians, we are called to be good stewards of the resources God has given us, including our money. This means being responsible for our spending, saving, and investing, and using our resources to glorify God and further His kingdom.

- Biblical principles for debt management - The Bible teaches us to avoid debt as much as possible and to be diligent in paying off any debt we have incurred. When we take on debt, we should do so responsibly and with a plan for paying it off.

- Money and giving in the Bible - The Bible teaches us to be generous with our money and to give to those in need. We are called to give sacrificially, not just out of our abundance, and to give joyfully, not grudgingly.

- The Christian perspective on saving and investing - The Bible encourages us to save for the future and to be wise in our investments. We should seek to use our resources to provide for ourselves and our families, but also to bless others and advance God's kingdom.

- Biblical wisdom on budgeting and financial planning - The Bible teaches us to be diligent in our financial planning and to budget wisely. We should seek to live within our means, avoid wasteful spending, and prioritize our financial resources according to God's priorities.

- The role of tithing in Christian stewardship - The Bible teaches us to tithe, or give 10% of our income, to support the work of God's kingdom. Tithing is not just a financial obligation, but a spiritual discipline that helps us grow in our faith and trust in God.

- Biblical teachings on generosity and charitable giving - The Bible encourages us to be generous and to give to those in need. We should seek to bless others with our financial resources, not just for their benefit, but also to bring glory to God.

- The connection between faith and finances in the Bible - The Bible teaches us that our faith and our finances are interconnected. We cannot separate our spiritual lives from our financial lives, and we should seek to honor God in both areas.

- Biblical advice on overcoming financial struggles - The Bible offers wisdom and encouragement for those who are facing financial struggles. We can trust in God's provision, seek wise counsel from others, and take practical steps to improve our financial situation.

- The significance of work and earning in the Bible - The Bible teaches us to work hard and to earn a living, but also to recognize that our ultimate source of provision is God. We should seek to use our work and our earnings to honor God and bless others.

- A Christian's guide to managing wealth and material possessions - The Bible offers guidance for how to manage our wealth and material possessions in a way that honors God. We should seek to be good stewards of what God has given us, using our resources to bless others and further His kingdom.

In conclusion, the Bible has much to say about financial stewardship, and as Christians, we have a responsibility to follow these principles and honor God with our money. May this book inspire and challenge you to grow in your financial stewardship and use your resources to bring glory to God.

Some Encouragement To Put Financial Stewardship Into Practice

As a Christian, you are called to be a good steward of the resources that God has entrusted to you. This means that you are responsible for managing your money wisely, using it to honor God and further His kingdom. It's not always easy to put financial stewardship into practice, but the rewards are worth it. Here are some words of encouragement to help you on your journey.

Foremost, remember that God is faithful. He promises to provide for your needs, and He will never leave you or forsake you. When you trust in Him and follow His principles, you can be confident that He will bless your efforts. Even if you face challenges or setbacks, you can trust that God is working all things together for your good.

Second, keep your focus on eternal values. It's easy to get caught up chasing wealth and material possessions, but these things are temporary. Instead, invest your time, energy, and resources in things that have lasting significance. Use your money to support ministries and organizations that are doing God's work, and be generous with those in need. Remember that true wealth is found in relationships, not in possessions.

Third, be intentional about your financial choices. You can't be a good steward by accident. You need to have a plan and stick to it. This means creating a budget that reflects your values and priorities, avoiding debt and making wise investments that align with your beliefs. It also means being accountable to others and seeking wise counsel when needed.

Finally, don't be afraid to take risks. God calls us to step out in faith and trust Him for the outcome. This may mean starting a business, pursuing an alternative career path, or giving sacrificially to a cause that is close to your heart. When you take risks for the sake of the kingdom, you are showing your faith in God's provision and His ability to use you in amazing ways.

In conclusion, putting financial stewardship into practice is a journey that requires commitment, discipline, and faith. But when you trust in God and follow His principles, you will experience His blessings and be able to make a difference in the world around you. So take heart and keep pressing on!

Final Thoughts And Encouragement

As we come to the end of this book, I hope that you have gained a deeper understanding and appreciation for the importance of financial stewardship in the Christian life. We have explored various aspects of biblical teachings on money, debt, giving, saving, investing, budgeting, tithing, generosity, work, and wealth management. This has been a journey of discovery and growth, and we trust that you have found it both enlightening and challenging.

It is important to remember that financial stewardship is not just about managing money, but it is also about managing our hearts and our relationship with God. As we learn to honor God with our finances, we also learn to surrender our lives to Him and trust Him to provide for our needs. This requires a great deal of faith, obedience, and sacrifice, but the rewards are immeasurable.

We encourage you to continue to study and apply biblical principles of financial stewardship in your daily life. Make it a habit to read and meditate on relevant scriptures and seek wise counsel from trusted Christian mentors. Use practical tools such as budgeting software, financial planners, and debt reduction plans to help you stay on track and achieve your financial goals.

Remember that financial stewardship is not just about accumulating wealth but also about using it for God's glory and the benefit of others. As we give generously and support worthy causes, we express our love for God and our compassion for those in need. We are called to be good stewards of all that God has entrusted to us, including our time, talents, and treasures.

In conclusion, let us strive to live a life of financial stewardship that honors God and blesses others. Let us trust in His provision, obey His commands, and seek His wisdom in all our financial decisions. May our hearts be filled with gratitude and generosity as we use our wealth to advance His kingdom and make a positive impact in the world. May God bless you abundantly as you seek to honor Him in every area of your life.

Terence's 10 key principles of Christian Financial Stewardship

With every book in this series, I hope that you as the reader gain knowledge that equips you for greater victory in the arena of finances. We have discussed various principles of Christian financial stewardship that you can implement in your personal and business finances.

Here are 10 key principles I consider being essential for fulfilling God's mandate to get money in the hands of his people. Here are the 10 Keys:

God owns everything: As Christians, we remember that all that we have comes from God, and we are only stewards of His resources.

Give generously: We are called to give generously to those in need and to support the work of the church and missions.

Live below your means: Living below your means allows you to save money, avoid debt, and have financial freedom.

Avoid debt: Debt can be a trap that keeps you from achieving financial freedom. Avoid it as much as possible.

Plan for the future: We must plan for our future needs, including retirement, emergency funds, and children's education.

Be content: Contentment is important in financial stewardship. It helps us avoid the temptation to overspend and be satisfied with what we have.

Seek wise counsel: Seek advice from trusted Christian financial experts, friends, and family to make wise financial decisions.

Use your money for God's Kingdom: Use your money to support God's work, mission, and charity, to advance His kingdom on earth.

Teach your children: Teach your children the principles of Christian financial stewardship from a young age, so they can grow up to be wise stewards of God's resources.

Trust in God: Ultimately, we must trust in God's provision and guidance in our financial journey.

These principles apply to various niches, whether you are a small business owner, family, young adult, retiree, or student. As Christians, we are called to be good stewards of all that God has given us. By implementing these principles, we can achieve financial freedom, support God's work, and glorify Him in all that we do.

Don't miss out!

Visit the website below and you can sign up to receive emails whenever Terence A. Townsend publishes a new book. There's no charge and no obligation.

https://books2read.com/r/B-A-SXLX-KRBUC

BOOKS 2 READ

Connecting independent readers to independent writers.

Did you love *God's Masterplan For Money - A Biblical Guide To Financial Stewardship*? Then you should read *The Power Of True Christian Virtue: Unleashing Your Full Potential*[1] by Terence A. Townsend!

"The Power of True Christian Virtue: Unleashing Your Full Potential" is a book that explores the transformative power of Christian virtues in one's personal and spiritual life. The book emphasizes the importance of cultivating virtues such as love, compassion, forgiveness, humility, and gratitude to unlock one's full potential and lead a fulfilling life.

Through a combination of personal anecdotes, biblical teachings, and practical advice, Mr. Townsend guides readers on a journey of self-discovery and spiritual growth. The book helps readers understand the significance of Christian virtues and how they can be applied to everyday life situations. It also provides insights into the obstacles that can hinder one's growth in virtues and how to overcome them.

1. https://books2read.com/u/4j5ke2

2. https://books2read.com/u/4j5ke2

The book's central message is that true Christian virtue is not just a set of moral principles to be followed, but a way of life that leads to personal transformation and fulfillment. By embracing Christian virtues and living them out in daily life, readers can tap into a deep reservoir of inner strength and joy, enabling them to live more purposeful and meaningful lives.

Overall, "The Power of True Christian Virtue: Unleashing Your Full Potential" is a powerful and inspiring guide to help readers deepen their faith and transform their lives through the practice of Christian virtues.

Read more at www.tefinancialservices.com.

Also by Terence A. Townsend

Healthy Eats Collection
Plant-Powered Mornings: 24 Delicious Vegan Breakfast Recipes to Start Your Day Right

The Christian Virtue Collection
The Power Of True Christian Virtue: Unleashing Your Full Potential

The Stewardship Collection
Power Of Financial Stewardship
God's Masterplan For Money - A Biblical Guide To Financial Stewardship

Watch for more at www.tefinancialservices.com.

About the Author

As an educator of financial stewardship, coach, speaker, and author, I want to help you take control of your finances and live a life of financial freedom. My goal is to educate as many people as possible about financial literacy and stewardship. There are a few ways you can work with me:

- Book me as a speaker for events, conferences, TED talks, and church meetings.

- Book me as a consultant to their company or business.

- You can also schedule a one-on-one appointment with me and/or my team.

- Register for one of our upcoming online courses.

I promote and discuss ways to improve one's financial literacy. I also teach about building a legacy for future generations. You can book me as a speaker for events, conferences, retreats and church meetings, or as a consultant to your company or business.

Thank you for reading this ebook on Christian Financial Stewardship. I hope that it has been helpful to you. Visit my website www.tefinancialservices.com for more information about me and my team. You can also follow me on Instagram at tefinacialservices.

Share this ebook with others and help empower them to build a legacy of stewardship for their families.

Read more at https://www.tefinancialservices.com.

About the Publisher

Townsend Enterprises Publishers produces high-quality, informative, and engaging books across various genres. With a commitment to excellence, the company has become a leading publisher of educational materials, including textbooks, workbooks, and instructional guides.

Founded in 2023, Townsend Enterprises Publishers has quickly become a trusted name in the publishing industry, with a reputation for providing top-notch editorial and design services. The company's team of experienced professionals includes editors, graphic designers, and marketing experts who work collaboratively to ensure that each publication meets the highest standards of quality and accuracy.

Townsend Enterprises Publishers offers a wide range of books that cater to diverse audiences, including students, educators, and professionals. From educational textbooks to self-help guides and inspirational works, the company's extensive catalogue provides something for everyone.

In addition to publishing books, Townsend Enterprises Publishers offers a range of additional services, such as editorial consultation, manuscript evaluation, and marketing support, to help aspiring authors and publishers bring their works to life.

With a dedication to excellence and a passion for empowering authors and readers alike, Townsend Enterprises Publishers is a publishing company that truly stands out in the industry.

www.ingramcontent.com/pod-product-compliance
Lightning Source LLC
Chambersburg PA
CBHW050405290526
45786CB00003B/1136

* 9 7 9 8 8 7 6 7 3 4 1 1 2 *